PRAYING THE PROMISES OF GOD SERIES (BOOK 1)

By His

Stripes

DANIEL C. OKPARA

God's Promises and Prayers for Healing

Copyright © October 2017 by Daniel C. Okpara.

All Rights Reserved. Contents of this book may not be reproduced in any way or by any means without written consent of the publisher, except for brief excerpts in critical reviews and articles.

Published By:

Better Life Media.

BETTER LIFE WORLD OUTREACH CENTER.

Website: www.BetterLifeWorld.org

Email: info@betterlifeworld.org

This title and others are available for quantity discounts for sale promotions, gifts, and evangelism. Visit our website or email us to get started.

Any scripture quotation in this book is taken from the King James Version or New International Version, except where stated. Used by permission.

All texts, calls, letters, testimonies, and inquiries are welcome.

Contents

FREE BONUS 6

Introduction: The Power of Praying God's Word Back to Him..7

Chapter 1: The Word Became Flesh.....................16

Chapter 2: Eight Ways to Pray God's Word Back to Him..22

Chapter 3: How to Pray for Healing.......................35

Chapter 4: God's Promises and Prayers for Healing..41

Chapter 5: General Healing Prayers.....................82

Get in Touch..100

Other Books By the Same Author......................101

About the Author..104

NOTES..106

"Forever, O LORD, Thy Word is settled in heaven." - Psalm 119:89

FREE BONUS ...

Download These 4 Powerful Books Today for FREE. Take Your Relationship With God to a New Level.

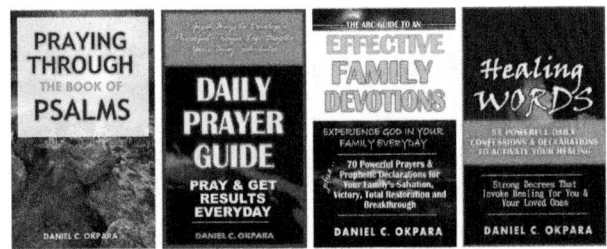

Go Here to Download:

www.betterlifeworld.org/grow

Introduction: The Power of Praying God's Word Back to Him

And this is the confidence that we have in him, that, if we ask anything according to his will, he heareth us: And if we know that he hear us, whatsoever we ask, we know that we have the petitions that we desired of him. - 1 John 5:14-15

The Bible instructs us to pray according to God's will. Many have asked on several occasions, *"How do I know I'm praying according to God's will?"*

There may be different answers, but one that we can take to the bank any day is that **"when we pray the Word of God back to Him, we are praying according to His will."** And as the scripture says, "we know that we will receive what we have asked of Him."

When Christ was confronted by Satan during His 40 days and nights fasting, He prayed the Word of God, and not human Words. Three times He said,

"It is written…"

The devil tried to persist, but finally gave up and ran away.

Then Jesus was led by the Holy Spirit into the wilderness to be tempted by the devil. 2 After He had gone without food for forty days and forty nights, He became hungry. 3 And the tempter came and said to Him,

"If You are the Son of God, command that these stones become bread."

₄ But Jesus replied, **"It is written and forever remains written, 'Man shall not live by bread alone, but by every word that comes out of the mouth of God.'"**

₅ Then the devil took Him into the holy city, Jerusalem, and placed Him on the pinnacle (highest point) of the temple.

₆ And he said [mockingly] to Him, "If You are the Son of God, throw Yourself down; for it is written,

'He will command His angels concerning You [to serve, care for, protect and watch over You]'; and 'They will lift you up on their hands, So that You will not strike Your foot against a stone.'"

₇Jesus said to him, "On the other hand, it is written and forever remains written, 'You shall not test the Lord your God.'"

₈ Again, the devil took Him up on a very high mountain and showed Him all the kingdoms of the world and the glory [splendor, magnificence, and excellence] of them; and he said to Him, "All these things I will give You, if You fall down and worship me."

₁₀ Then Jesus said to him, **"Go away, Satan! For it is written and forever remains written, 'You shall worship the Lord your God, and serve Him only.'"**

Then the devil left Him; and angels came and ministered to Him, bringing Him food and serving Him- Matt 4:1-11

This is the template for overcoming the devil in any area that he attacks us. If our health is attacked, we find scriptures and God's promises regarding our health and continue to pray them until our total restoration. If our finances are attacked, we locate scriptures and promises on our finances and pray them until our blessings show forth. The same thing applies to other areas of life.

It looks simple, right?

Sure, it does. And as humans, we always have a problem when spiritual realities look simple. We want things to be a bit complicated and technical. Fortunately, the simplicity of God's ways does not reduce the potency to change lives and produce great transformations.

ıd Bible promises. Then pray them without ceasing until they become manifest in your life. It's simple but effective.

In John 15:7, Jesus said, "If you abide in me, and my words abide in you, ye shall ask what ye will, and it shall be done unto you."

The Amplified Bible puts that verse this way, "If you remain in Me and My words remain in you [that is, if we are vitally united and My message lives in your heart], ask whatever you wish and it will be done for you."

That's simply saying, "Take some time first and read the Words of God. Then meditate on them. After that, pray, and your prayers will be answered."

I've found out over the years that in prayers, it's what the WORD of God says that really matters, not what we are saying. Praying with words like, **"LORD, You said"** is much more important than any other.

In Genesis 31:3, God makes a promise to Jacob, saying, "I will be with you." That is, "I will deal well with you."

Then later, when in terrible crises, Jacob cries out to God in prayer and reminds Him of his promise to him. He says:

"O God of my father Abraham, and God of my father Isaac, the Lord which saidst unto me, Return unto thy country, and to thy kindred, and I will deal well with thee... (Gen 32:9-12)

He reminded God His promises.

The fuel of prayer is the promises of God. We remind God in prayer of what He has said and call Him to be faithful to His Word. That is the very backbone of all faith-filled praying - The promises of God.

"For all the promises of God in him are yea, and in him Amen, unto the glory of God by us." - 2 Cor. 1:20

The promises of God have the power to defeat any adverse situation that life throws at you. The promises can overcome any attack that comes your way – be it in your mind, in your body, in your home, in your office – anywhere.

The promises of God are not dismissive, casual promises such as we often make; they are rock-solid, unequivocal, commitments made by God Himself. Because God is faithful, we can have full assurance that what God has promised will indeed happen.

As you read these Bible verses about the promises of God, claim them over your life! Memorize the Scriptures that promise to overcome what you are facing today. Pray them over and over; speak them out loud from time to time, and you will begin to see God move in your life.

Chapter 1: The Word Became Flesh

"In the beginning was the Word, and the Word was with God, and the Word was God. The same was in the beginning with God.

"And the Word was made flesh, and dwelt among us, (and we beheld his glory, the glory as of the only begotten of the Father,) full of grace and truth." - John 1:1, 14

Before the birth of Christ, an angel (Gabriel) came with a message from God to Mary. He gave her a WORD from God, saying:

"Do not be afraid, Mary, for you have found favor with God. Listen carefully: you will conceive in your womb and give birth to a son, and you shall name Him Jesus.

He will be great and eminent and will be called the Son of the Most High; and the Lord God will give Him the throne of His father David.

And He will reign over the house of Jacob (Israel) forever, and of His kingdom there shall be no end" - Luke 1:30-33 – (AMP).

Mary asked how's that going to happen since she was a virgin. The angel assured her that the Holy Spirit will brood on the WORD she had just been told.

"Then Mary said, "Behold, I am the servant of the Lord; may it be done to me according to your word."

And the angel left her.

Mary believed the WORD that the angel gave. "And the WORD became flesh and dwelt among us, and we beheld His glory, the glory as of the only begotten of the Father, full of grace and truth" (John 1:14).

"It's right to say that the WORD that was spoken to Mary which she believed was what formed flesh in her as the "only begotten of the Father."

If Mary had said, "No, I don't want this."

Or, "Sorry, I'm not going to take this. The world will make jest of me."

If that had been her response, I'm sure heaven would have looked for someone else to extend that favor to. But thank God she believed the WORD, "and the WORD became flesh and dwelt among us."

The message I am trying to pass is this:

When we believe the WORD, pray the WORD, and confess the WORD, it has power to turn the most impossible situation around.

Yes, "...the word of God is living and active and full of power [making it operative, energizing, and effective]. It is sharper than any two-edged sword, penetrating as far as the division of the soul and spirit [the completeness of a person], and of both joints and marrow [the deepest parts of our nature], exposing and judging the very thoughts and intentions of the heart (Heb. 4:12 – AMP).

The WORD of God - the promises of God for any situation - which you read, believe and pray - works in your spirit, soul, body, marrows and bones, and causes the realities of God to be made manifest in your life.

The WORD can turn even dead situations around. The WORD brings healing to your spirit, soul, mind, physical body and your loved ones.

Daniel C. Okpara

"Praying the Word of God – the promises of God – for any situation - will invoke the Glory of God and change any situation, because God is inseparable from His WORD."

Chapter 2: Eight Ways to Pray God's Word Back to Him

There are promises that cover whatever area of challenge you may be currently facing. Do you need healing? Wisdom? The ability to pay the bills?

Whatever it is, you can pray one of God's promises that relate to your issue, and hold onto it. This entire series – Praying the Promises of God – is intended to bring you God's promises for many different situations.

Here are eight ways to pray these promises back to God.

1. Find the Promises that Relate to Your Situation.

I read a story that challenged me a lot some years ago. It was about the wife of a man of God who fell sick and was told by doctors that she had only few days to live. Her husband, a preacher, prayed and prayed and invited other men of God to pray, yet nothing happened. Her case continued to deteriorate.

Eventually, the woman mustered some strength, settled down and located forty scriptures on God's health and healing plan.

As she continued to read and meditate on them, and minister to herself with those scriptures, she was miraculously healed.

> *"The Word of God carries life. It is the Power of God in a book."*

The first thing to do before praying about any situation is to locate God's Words and promises about that situation. Make a compilation of verses that speak on those areas, and then begin to do battle with those scriptures.

2. Meditate on the promises

"This Book of the Law shall not depart from your mouth, but you shall read [and meditate on] it day and night, so that you may be careful to do [everything] in accordance with all that is written in it; for then you will make your way prosperous,

and then you will be successful" - *Joshua 1:8 (AMP)*

To meditate means to think deeply and carefully about something for a period. Focus your mind on the promise that you are trusting God for, and reflect on the WORD for a while. Let the truths permeate your soul. Then you'll see how great a God you serve!

3. Personalize the Promises in Prayers

Take the promises you read and make them yours.

For example, if you are praying for healing and you read somewhere like Isaiah 53:5 which says: "But he was wounded for our transgressions, he was bruised for our iniquities: the chastisement of our peace was upon him; and with his stripes we are healed."

Personalizing this scripture, you'll begin to pray, say,

"LORD Jesus, You were wounded for my transgressions, bruised for my iniquities, chastised that I may have peace, and by Your stripes, I am healed. So I claim my healing this day, in Jesus name"

The same thing applies to any other area you are looking forward to a divine intervention:

Locate the scriptures that promise you deliverance on your situation, meditate on the scriptures, personalize them and begin to do battle with them.

---

4. Declare the Promises Daily in Faith

But what saith it? The word is nigh thee, even in thy mouth, and in thy heart: that is, the word of faith, which we preach;

That if thou shalt confess with thy mouth the Lord Jesus, and shalt believe in thine heart that God hath raised him from the dead, thou shalt be saved.

For with the heart man believeth unto righteousness, and with the mouth confession is made unto salvation. - Rom 10:8-10

Verse 9 says that if you "confess with thy mouth the Lord Jesus, and shalt believe in thine heart that God hath raised him from the dead, thou shalt be saved."

Jesus Christ is the Word of God. So that's simply saying, *"If you confess the Word of God and believe that the Word is greater than your situations, you'll be saved from those situations."*

2 Corinthians 4:13 says, "It is written: 'I believed; therefore, I have spoken.' Since we have that same spirit of faith, we also believe and therefore speak."

In other words, through faith confession, one can lay claim and receive the promise of God. Talk or confess the Word till it becomes a reality for you.

Our words are like seeds. What we speak determines what we eventually see as harvest. This was the reason Abram's name was changed to Abraham so it can register in his spirit that he was a father of many nations even when he had no son.

You can't afford to be careless with your tongue and expect to live in the blessings of God. "For by your words you will be acquitted, and by your words you will be condemned" (Matthew 12:37).

Don't dwell on the magnitude of the situation, or what experts have said. Continue to declare the Word of God regarding your situation by faith. Your change will surely take place.

5. Pray in the Holy Ghost

In the same way, the Spirit helps us in our weakness. We do not know what we ought to pray for, but the Spirit himself intercedes for us through wordless groans.

And he who searches our hearts knows the mind of the Spirit because the Spirit intercedes for God's people in accordance with the will of God. (Rom 8:26-27)

The Holy Spirit is given to help us in our weakness. When we pray in the Holy Ghost, the Spirit is helping us pray. And the spirit of God cannot pray amiss, but in the very will of God.

Sometimes one is not able to express himself adequately by words in prayer, considering the enormity of the need to be met. That is the time to turn it over to the Lord by praying in the Spirit.

This is what you do. You read the promise or promises out loud and say, "LORD, I'm praying and receiving these promises into my life. Holy Spirit, please take over right now. Help me pray these Words through, in Jesus name."

Praying in other tongues is a great blessing for us. It empowers our prayers to be in God's will. If you're baptized with the Holy Spirit with the evidence of speaking in other tongues, then allow the Holy Spirit to pray through you this way. However, this is not mandatory. Speaking and praying the promises of God in any way, by uttering it, works

6. Sing the Promises

Let the people praise thee, O God; let all the people praise thee. O let the nations be glad and sing for joy: for thou shalt judge the people righteously, and govern the nations upon earth. Selah.

Let the people praise thee, O God; let all the people praise thee. Then shall the earth yield her increase; and God, even our own God, shall bless us. God shall bless us, and

all the ends of the earth shall fear him. - Psalm 67:3-7

Praise is a powerful means of claiming God's promises. When praise goes up, blessings come down.

One way you can pray the promises of God is to praise God for the promises you are praying for, declaring and believing.

You'll find in scripture that in tough times, the people of God were instructed to turn to praise with all manner of instruments. And as they did, God's heavenly army appears on the scene and gives them victory.

You can turn a particular verse or verses into songs and sing them back to God. Singing God's promises is also a way to pray the promises of God.

7. Exercise Patience

"You need to persevere so that when you have done the will of God, you will receive what he has promised. For in just a little while, he who is coming will come and will not delay. But my righteous one will live by faith. And I take no pleasure in the one who shrinks back" - Heb 10:36-39.

Why do we need to have patience? Because some promises might take some time before they manifest. There can be various reasons why, either known or unknown. Regardless of what your situation looks like today, remember that He is faithful, and He has promised never to leave or forsake you.

8. Take Steps of Faith

While exercising patience, we must learn to take steps of faith towards what we are praying and believing God for. For "Just as the body is dead when there is no spirit in it, so faith is dead if it is not the kind that results in good deeds." (James 2:26).

James is not saying that our works make us righteous before God, but that real saving faith is demonstrated by doing something. For example, if you are praying for healing, start taking gradual actions of faith. You actions of faith are also as important as your prayers of faith.

Chapter 3: How to Pray for Healing

"God wants you to be healed and live a healthy life. Do not accept anything contrary to that"

When praying for healing, there are a few things you can do:

Call the Elders of the Church to Pray With You

Is anyone sick? He should call for the elders of the church and they should pray over him and pour a little oil upon him, calling on the Lord to heal him. And their prayer, if offered in faith, will heal him, for the Lord will make him well; and if his sickness was caused by some sin, the Lord will forgive him - James 5:14-15 (TLB)

Here, the Apostle James is trying to re-emphasize the Words of Christ that "...if two believers on earth agree [that is, are of one mind, in harmony] about anything that they ask [within the will of God], it will be done for them by My Father in heaven." - Matt 18:19 (AMP).

So elders of the church refers to other believers in the faith. They may not necessarily be ordained pastors or church elders. Neither must they be people of the same denomination. Provided these are believers with **the fear of the LORD**, (not necessarily people prophesying and seeing visions), call them to pray with you, or your loved ones.

Applying the prayer of agreement is one way you can pray for healing for yourself and for your loved ones

Anoint Yourself Daily

No one can pray for you the way you will pray for yourself. You're the biggest prophet of your life. Jesus said that whatever you forbid here on earth will be forbidden in heaven, and whatever you allow will be allowed. So, to activate your healing, continue to pray and anoint yourself daily.

Administer the Holy Communion Daily

"Then Jesus said unto them, 'Verily, verily, I say unto you, Except ye eat the flesh of the Son of man, and drink his blood, ye have no life in you.

"Whoso eateth my flesh, and drinketh my blood, hath eternal life; and I will raise him up at the last day.

For my flesh is meat indeed, and my blood is drink indeed.

"He that eateth my flesh, and drinketh my blood, dwelleth in me, and I in him.

"As the living Father hath sent me, and I live by the Father: so he that eateth me, even he shall live by me.

"This is that bread which came down from heaven: not as your fathers did eat manna, and are dead: he that eateth of this bread shall live forever" - John 6: 53-58

Jesus was talking about believing in Him and accepting Him as the LORD and Savior here. But the Words He used to explain that also shows us what happens when we take the Holy Communion.

The Holy Communion is not just an every Sunday or Wednesday ritual meant to remind us of the death of Christ. While that is the primary purpose, it is also an instrument of exercising authority over the devil.

When we take the Holy Communion, we are united with the LORD in His death and resurrection. We die to sin (and its consequences - sickness, oppression and death) and resurrect to righteousness (and its benefits - eternal life, health and peace of mind).

Yes, it may not sound like what you've heard, but the body and blood of Jesus Christ is a mystery that restores our health for today and eternity. Apart from waiting to take the communion in Church service, you can regularly prepare and take this spiritual meal on your own, and use it as a point of contact to claim your healing, deliverance and total restoration.

> *For as often as ye eat this bread, and drink this cup, ye do shew the Lord's death till he come.* - 1 Corinthians 11:26

You could just get anything (for bread and wine elements) that will represent the body and the blood of Christ. Then pray over it and take it every day, decreeing your unity in the death of Christ and His resurrection.

No devil can withstand the reality of the death and resurrection of Christ and our victory through it.

Chapter 4: God's Promises and Prayers for Healing

There are dozens of God's promises for healing. The ones listed here are in no way exhaustive. As you go through these scriptures, and the corresponding prayers...

1. Find comfort in them

2. Meditate on the promises that go with each prayer.

3. Mutter the promises to yourself, sing them out, let your heart confess and memorize them.

4. Pray the corresponding prayers in faith.

The prayers are prepared as if you were praying for yourself. The words, "*I, myself*" are used as a personal pronoun to identify that you are praying for yourself. But you can use the prayers to intercede for someone else privately, or to pray a prayer of agreement with the person. Where this is the case, simply replace the identifications of ***"myself"*** to the person's name.

I recommend that you pray these prayers as many times as possible and believe God for healing.

You may need to pray the prayers for several days, weeks or months. Don't give up. When we pray and confess the WORD OF GOD over our lives, we are sure of victory. It is only a matter of time.

Remember that the ultimate goal of any sickness in your body is to destroy you. But God's ultimate plan through Christ is for you to live in peace and sound health. So you should continue to reject that sickness and give it a hard fight, and refuse to accept anything other than perfect health.

Prayer 1: Forgive and Heal Me O LORD

Promise

Psalm 103:2-5 (TLB) - Yes, I will bless the Lord and not forget the glorious things he does for me.

He forgives all my sins. He heals me.

He ransoms me from hell. He surrounds me with loving-kindness and tender mercies.

He fills my life with good things! My youth is renewed like the eagle's!

2 Chronicles 7:14 - If my people, which are called by my name, shall humble themselves, and pray, and seek my face, and turn from their wicked ways; then will I

hear from heaven, and will forgive their sin, and will heal their land.

Prayer

Heavenly Father, I come to You this day according to Thy Word.

I humble myself and confess my sins before Thee.

Indeed, if I say that I have not sinned, I deceive myself and the truth is not in me.

LORD, I now confess my sins before THEE (Confess your sins).

I confess my sins of lust, gluttony, evil desires, jealously, hatred and neglect of Your instructions.

O LORD, please forgive me today and cleanse me with the Blood of Jesus Christ.

Look upon me with mercy and let Your love shine upon my heart.

I confess that Jesus Christ is my LORD and personal Savior.

I give You my life LORD Jesus. Come and make your home in my heart.

In any way I have sinned and opened up myself for this sickness to torment me, LORD, please forgive and heal me.

Your Word says that if we humble ourselves and confess our sins and repent, that You forgive and heal our lands.

LORD, I ask You right now to forgive and heal me. Deliver me from pains and redeem me from the grave.

Let Your loving kindness and mercies surround me from this day forward.

Fill my life with good things and renew my strength.

In Jesus name I pray.

Prayer 2: Free from Bitterness

Promise

Mark 11: 25-26 - And when ye stand praying, forgive, if ye have ought against any: that your Father also which is in heaven may forgive you your trespasses.

But if ye do not forgive, neither will your Father which is in heaven forgive your trespasses.

Matthew 18:21-22 (AMP) - Then Peter came to Him and asked, "Lord, how many times will my brother sin against me and I forgive him and let it go? Up to seven times?" Jesus answered him, "I say to you, not up to seven times, but seventy times seven.

Luke 6:27(AMP) - "But I say to you who hear Me and pay attention to My words: Love [that is, unselfishly seek the best or higher good for] your enemies, make it a practice to do good to those who hate you.

Colossians 3:12-13(AMP) - So, as God's own chosen people, who are holy, set apart, sanctified for His purpose and well-beloved [by God Himself], put on a heart of compassion, kindness, humility, gentleness, and patience [which has the power to endure whatever injustice or unpleasantness comes, with good temper]; bearing graciously with one another, and willingly forgiving each other if one has a cause for complaint against another; just as the Lord has forgiven you, so should you forgive.

Prayer

My Father My Father, Maker of heaven and earth.

I thank You for the gift of forgiveness.

You forgave me even when I do not know it, made me Your child, and a partaker of the covenant of life.

Through Christ You gave me access to Your heavenly blessings, not minding or counting on my trespasses.

I thank You sincerely for this love. May You be praised forever and ever.

Father, I have read Your Word and do accept that forgiveness is Your will. I accept that You want us to forgive others and let their offenses go.

LORD, I ask You for grace and help to forgive everyone that I hold anything against. I ask You for grace to practice advance forgiveness henceforth.

You know I feel bad about the ways these people have treated me. To be honest, I am not happy about their attitude.

But LORD, I have to let this go.

Please take the bitterness and anger that I feel in my heart and pour Your grace and kindness in my spirit from this day onwards.

Help me to genuinely forgive ....(name the persons).

I now pray for their welfare. LORD, help them to become who you want them to be.

Let Your light shine on their ways. Bring them closer to Your Light every day, in Jesus name.

O LORD, whatever pain, sickness or affliction in my life as a result of bitterness and unforgiveness, Heavenly Father, please heal me of them right now.

As I let every form of bitterness, resentment, anger and grudges go this day, LORD, I receive Your healing in my spirit, soul and body.

In Jesus name.

Prayer 3: Healing is God's Will

Promise

Matthew 8:2-3 - A man with leprosy came and knelt before him and said, "Lord, if you are willing, you can make me clean."

Jesus reached out his hand and touched the man. "I am willing," he said. "Be clean!" Immediately he was cleansed of his leprosy

3 John 2 (AMP) - Beloved, I pray that in every way you may succeed and prosper and be in good health [physically], just as [I know] your soul prospers [spiritually].

Acts 10:38 (AMP) - How God anointed Jesus of Nazareth with the Holy Spirit and with great power; and He went around doing good and healing all who were oppressed by the devil, because God was with Him

Matthew 9:35 (NIV) - Jesus went through all the towns and villages, teaching in their synagogues, proclaiming the good news of the kingdom and healing every disease and sickness.

Matthew 14:14 - When Jesus landed and saw a large crowd, he had compassion on them and healed their sick.

Matthew 4:23 - Jesus went throughout Galilee, teaching in their synagogues, preaching the gospel of the kingdom, and healing every disease and sickness among the people.

Prayer

Father LORD in Heaven, it is Your will for us to be healed. While You were on Earth through Jesus Christ, You went about doing good and healing all that were oppressed.

In many places, You had compassion on the sick and healed them. You made it very clear to those who came to You and asked that it is Your will for us to be healed and live a healthy life.

LORD, look at those scriptures. Look at them.

According to Romans 15:4, whatever is written in scriptures was written for our instruction, so that through patience and the encouragement we might have hope and overflow with confidence in the promises.

LORD, I am confident in Thy promises of healing. You did it before, You are doing it today. You will do it in my life.

You are the same, yesterday, today and forever.

Therefore, LORD, I ask You right now to heal me.

Let Your healing hand stretch through to my body right now and touch me. In Jesus name.

Thank You LORD Jesus for my healing.

Prayer 4: Healing is in the Covenant - None of These Diseases

Promise

Exodus 23:25-26 (AMP) - You shall serve only the Lord your God, and He shall bless your bread and water. I will also remove sickness from among you.

No one shall suffer miscarriage or be barren in your land; I will fulfill the number of your days

Deuteronomy 7:12-16 - Wherefore it shall come to pass, if ye hearken to these judgments, and keep, and do them, that the Lord thy God shall keep unto thee the covenant and the mercy which he sware unto thy fathers:

And he will love thee, and bless thee, and multiply thee: he will also bless the fruit of thy womb, and the fruit of thy land, thy corn, and thy wine, and thine oil, the increase of thy kine, and the flocks of thy sheep, in the land which he sware unto thy fathers to give thee.

Thou shalt be blessed above all people: there shall not be male or female barren among you, or among your cattle.

And the Lord will take away from thee all sickness, and will put none of the evil diseases of Egypt, which thou knowest, upon thee; but will lay them upon all them that hate thee.

Prayer

Heavenly Father, I thank You for Your covenant of health and healing. You are ever true and Your Words are certain.

I declare that I am a child of God through Jesus. For it is written in Galatians 3:26-29 that we are children of God through faith in Christ and are Abraham's seed, and heirs according to the promise.

Therefore, LORD, Your covenant of health and promise to take sickness away is for me, my family and friends.

According to the covenant and promise, none of the diseases that I read and hear about in the world, which represents Egypt today, shall afflict me.

O LORD, I put You in remembrance of Thy WORD this day. As I've read in Exodus

23:25-26, You said that as we serve Thee, You will bless our bread and water, and take sickness away from us.

You said that we shall not be barren or have miscarriage, and that You will cause us to fulfill our days.

Lord, this is what You said and I am reminding You of this Word. Take this sickness away from me this day.

Cause Your healing, blessings and peace to manifest in my body henceforth. Bless my bread and water and take away any kind of defilement from my system.

Let the Blood of Jesus Christ flow into my system right now and flush every kind of germs, bacteria, virus and disease out of my body.

In Jesus name.

Prayer 5: Jesus Was Wounded for Our Healing

Promise

1 Peter 2:23-24 (AMP) - While being reviled and insulted, He did not revile or insult in return; while suffering, He made no threats [of vengeance], but kept entrusting Himself to Him who judges fairly.

He personally carried our sins in His body on the cross [willingly offering Himself on it, as on an altar of sacrifice], so that we might die to sin [becoming immune from the penalty and power of sin] and live for righteousness; for by His wounds you [who believe] have been healed"

Isaiah 53:3-5 (AMP) - He was despised and rejected by men, A Man of sorrows and pain and acquainted with grief; And like One from whom men hide their faces. He was despised, and we did not appreciate His worth or esteem Him.

But [in fact] He has borne our griefs, And He has carried our sorrows and pains; Yet we [ignorantly] assumed that He was stricken, Struck down by God and degraded and humiliated [by Him].

But He was wounded for our transgressions, He was crushed for our wickedness [our sin, our injustice, our wrongdoing]; The punishment [required] for our well-being fell on Him, And by His stripes (wounds) we are healed.

Prayer

Heavenly Father, I thank You for sending Jesus Christ, Your only begotten Son to die for me.

According to Thy WORD, He personally carried our sins in His body on the cross, so that we might die to sin and live for righteousness; He carried our sorrows and pains. He was wounded for our disobediences, He was crushed for our badness, The punishment for our sins fell on Him; And by His stripes (wounds) we are healed.

LORD Jesus, I thank You for carrying my sins, sorrows and pains in Your own body at the Cross.

Yeah, by Your stripes I am healed.

I was healed at the cross when Jesus Christ died there. Therefore, no sickness or pain has any more power over my life.

I hereby declare my healing through the death of Jesus Christ.

I confess that I am haled.

I command every sickness and pain in my life this moment to seize.

I command my body to receive healing, strength and total restoration,

In Jesus name I pray.

Prayer 6: Bind Up My Wounds O Lord

Promise

Psalm 34:20 - For the LORD protects the bones of the righteous; not one of them is broken!

Psalm 41:3 - The LORD will sustain him upon his sickbed; In his illness, You restore him to health.

Psalm 147:3 - He heals the brokenhearted and binds up their wounds.

Jeremiah 30:17 - For I will restore health to you, and your wounds I will heal, declares the Lord.

Prayer

O LORD, please sustain me in faith, all through this period, as You are restoring my health. Engrave my heart with peace and faith to continue to trust and believe in the infallibility of Thy Words.

Heal my heart of all fears and brokenness and bind up my injuries.

Heal my frames and wounds, and protect my bones from being broken, according to Thy Word

In Jesus name I pray.

Prayer 7: Grace to Obey the Holy Spirit

Promise

Exodus 15:26 (AMP) - "...If you will diligently listen and pay attention to the voice of the Lord your God, and do what is right in His sight, and listen to His commandments, and keep [foremost in your thoughts and actively obey] all His precepts and statutes, then I will not put on you any of the diseases which I have put on the Egyptians; for I am the Lord who heals you.

Prayer

Heavenly Father, the Father of Love and Mercy.

I ask You to forgive me in any way I have lived in disobediences regarding my health. Forgive me where I have done things that are wrong and disregarded Your commandments.

I ask for grace this day to truly repent of behaviors that displeases You, and behaviors that open doors to diseases and sickness.

Deliver me from any curse or sickness operating in my life as a result of my disobedience in any way.

Holy Spirit, I call upon You to help me from now onwards to be more obedient to You. Help me to pay attention and understand what You are asking me to do per time and to do it.

If there is anything I need to do in any way to manifest my healing, even as I pray, believe and wait, please Holy Spirit, show them to me.

Henceforth, I declare my willingness to obey You Holy Spirit.

Baptize me with grace for obedience.

In Jesus name I pray

Prayer 8: Speaking to The Mountain, healing the sick

Promise

Mark 11:23-26 - For verily I say unto you, That whosoever shall say unto this mountain, Be thou removed, and be thou cast into the sea; and shall not doubt in his heart, but shall believe that those things which he saith shall come to pass; he shall have whatsoever he saith.

Therefore I say unto you, What things soever ye desire, when ye pray, believe that ye receive them, and ye shall have them.

And when ye stand praying, forgive, if ye have ought against any: that your Father also which is in heaven may forgive you your trespasses.

But if ye do not forgive, neither will your Father which is in heaven forgive your trespasses.

Mark 16:16-18 (AMP) - "He who has believed [in Me] and has been baptized will be saved [from the penalty of God's wrath and judgment]; but he who has not believed will be condemned.

These signs will accompany those who have believed: in My name they will cast out demons, they will speak in new tongues; They will pick up serpents, and if they drink anything deadly, it will not hurt them; they will lay hands on the sick, and they will get well."

Matthew 10:8 - Heal the sick, raise the dead, cleanse those who have leprosy, drive out demons. Freely you have received; freely give

---

Prayer

Almighty Father, I thank You for the authority You have given me in Christ Jesus to speak to mountains, situations and challenges and see them leave.

Your Word says I should heal the sick, cast out devils, raise the dead, bless others, and speak with new tongues.

O LORD, I am exercising this authority right now.

I lay my hand upon myself this moment and I command this sickness in my body to leave.

As it is written, "whatever I bind, forbid, declare to be improper and unlawful on earth shall be bound in heaven, and whatever I loose, permit, declare lawful on earth shall be loosed in heaven" (Matthew 18:18)

It is also written that I shall decree a thing and it shall be established, and light will shine on my ways (Job 22:28).

O LORD, I stand on Your Word this day and forbid this sickness in my life. I declare this sickness improper and unlawful from today onwards.

I command the roots of this sickness to wither by fire right now, in Jesus name

I command myself to be healed.

I arrest every seed of diseases in my body. I command them to be destroyed right now.

Holy Ghost fire, move into my body right now.

I set myself free from any form of sickness this moment.

I command strength to flow into my system.

And I command my body to be restored this day.

In Jesus name I pray.

Prayer 9: Strengthen Me O LORD

Promise

Isaiah 41:10 (TLB) - Fear not, for I am with you. Do not be dismayed. I am your God. I will strengthen you; I will help you; I will uphold you with my victorious right hand

Matthew 11:28 - Come unto me, all ye that labour and are heavy laden, and I will give you rest.

Psalm 107:19-21 (AMP) - Then they cried out to the Lord in their trouble, and He saved them from their distresses. He sent His word and healed them, And rescued them from their destruction. Let them give thanks to the Lord for His lovingkindness, And for His wonderful acts to the children of men!

Psalm 18:3: I call upon the LORD, who is worthy to be praised, And I am saved from my enemies.

Psalm 34:4, 6, 17, 19 - I sought the LORD, and He answered me, And delivered me from all my fears.

This poor man called, and the LORD heard him; he saved him out of all his troubles.

The righteous cry, and the LORD hears And delivers them out of all their troubles.

Many are the afflictions of the righteous, But the LORD delivers him out of them all.

Prayer

Father, in the Name of Jesus Christ, I thank You for Your promise to strengthen me, help me and be with me. I thank You for Your willingness to uphold me and give me rest.

O LORD, I come to You this moment and pray that You take away all forms of fear from my heart. Fill me with Your love, power and sound mind.

Strengthen my inner man, and revive my optimism.

Holy Spirit, take away every form of heavy burden in my spirit and fill me with the assurance of Your presence. I enter into the rest that God has promised me from today forward.

I declare that I shall not die. I shall live and declare the goodness of God in the land of the living.

I declare that God has delivered me from all my troubles and pains and given me rest and peace.

In Jesus name.

Prayer 10: Anoint the Sick With Oil - The Anointing Breaks the Yoke

Promise

Acts 28:8 - The father of Publius was sick in bed, suffering from fever and dysentery. Paul went in to see him, and after praying and placing his hands on him, he healed the man.

Isaiah 10:27 - And it shall come to pass in that day, that his burden shall be taken away from off thy shoulder and his yoke from off thy neck, and the yoke shall be destroyed because of the anointing.

James 5:14-15 (AMP) - Is anyone among you sick? He must call for the elders (spiritual leaders) of the church and they are to pray over him, anointing him with oil in the name of the Lord; and the prayer of faith will restore the one who is sick, and the Lord will raise him up; and if he has committed sins, he will be forgiven.

Mark 6:13 - They also drove out many demons and healed many of the sick, anointing them with oil.

Prayer

Heavenly Father, I anoint myself this day according to Thy Word.

I declare that I am in agreement with You, Thy Word and the Holy Spirit. "For there are three that bear record in heaven, the Father, the Word, and the Holy Ghost: and these three are one (1 John 5:7).

By this anointing LORD, I ask that the Power of the Holy Spirit will move into every part of my body right now. I pray that every yoke of sickness in my life be destroyed this moment.

As it is written, to "anoint the sick with oil in the name of the Lord; and the prayer of faith will restore the one who is sick."

I anoint myself and pray the prayer of faith, in the name of Jesus Christ. I command a complete restoration of my health this moment. I declare myself saved healed from this affliction.

In Jesus name

Chapter 5: General Healing Prayers

These prayers are culled from my other books on healing:

1. How to Exercise Authority Over Sickness

2. Healing Prayers

3. Healing Words

As God gives me revelation about sickness and healing, I pen them down and bring them to God's people.

These tools are intended to help you **eat God's Words on healing,** develop faith to receive and manifest your healing, and use them to do battle against any sickness in your body.

I recommend that you get these materials and let God speak to you through them.

There are about 30 prayer points in this chapter, all designed to help you pray for healing for yourself and for your loved ones.

SECTION 1: **PERSONAL PRAYERS FOR HEALING.**

---

1. *Heavenly Father, I come to you in humility and thank You, for it is Your will that I should be in good health.*

I know that You are not the one afflicting me with sickness and pain.

Yes, LORD. This sickness and pain is not from You.

You did not allow Your Son, Jesus Christ, to be flogged and to die for my salvation and health, only to come back and start afflicting me again.

Not at all

Father, I know that this pain and sickness is from the devil, the evil one.

But I thank You also because You have made adequate provision for me to be healed and delivered from this sickness and to walk in divine health.

My praise and thanks is unto THEE forever and ever, in Jesus name.

---

2. Heavenly Father, I agree that I have not been faithful and righteous as You want from me in the past. I know I have done so many evil things that opened the door for this sickness to come on me.

But now, LORD, I ask You to Forgive me of those wrongs and evils.

According to Your Word in 2 Chronicles 7:14, I humble myself and confess my sins before THEE. LORD, please forgive me and heal my spirit, soul and body this day, in Jesus Name.

---

3. By the blood of Jesus, I receive forgiveness of sin and cleansing from all unrighteousness. Now, OLORD, I come to the throne of grace cleansed by the precious blood of Jesus.

I confess that I am sanctified by the Blood of Jesus Christ. I am healed by the Blood of Jesus. I overcome weakness and sickness of the body by the blood of Jesus. I overcome Satan and his demons by the Blood of Jesus, in Jesus name

---

4. Father LORD, once again I pray, root out every seed of unforgivenes and bitterness in me

Give me grace to forgive anyone who has offended me in the past.

I declare today and from now onwards that I hold nothing against anyone. I forgive everyone and receive my healing in Jesus name.

---

5. In the name of Jesus Christ, I release these ones (Mention names) who I have something against.

I release them from my heart today and commit them to THEE O Lord.

Give me grace LORD to walk in obedience, forgiveness and peace of mind henceforth and be a light and salt to others, even those who willfully offend me, in Jesus name.

6. *Heavenly Father, I know that sometimes sickness is caused by abusing our bodies and not caring for ourselves enough.*

LORD, I therefore pray today and ask that You give me grace to take care of my body henceforth.

I believe Your Word that my body is the temple of the Holy Spirit.

O LORD, destroy every urge of carelessness, over eating, gluttony and love of food in my life.

Food is made for man and not man for food.

I claim my victory over my appetite this day and decree that henceforth, my eating and drinking will glorify God, in Jesus name.

7. *Father in heaven, Jesus said in Matthew 15:13 that 'Every plant, which my heavenly Father hath not planted, shall be rooted up'. Therefore, I root out every evil seed of sickness in my body right now, In Jesus name.*

---

8. *Whatever I have eaten, willingly or unwillingly, spiritually or physically, that is causing sickness in my body, be destroyed by fire right now, In Jesus name.*

---

9. *Any man or woman, spiritually or physically, projecting weakness, sickness, malaria, High Blood Pressure, pain (mention what is happening to You) against me, be arrested, frustrated and crippled by fire right now, in Jesus name.*

10. Every spirit responsible for this sickness (name it), I dare you with God's Word. My body is the temple of the Holy Spirit. You have no right in my body and system. Therefore, I command you to get out of this body and get down into abyss in Jesus name.

11. It is written:

"But He was wounded for our transgressions, He was bruised for our iniquities; the chastisement of our peace was upon Him, and by His stripes we are healed." - **Isaiah 53:5.**

"Who his own self bare our sins in his own body on the tree that we, being dead to sins, should live unto righteousness: by whose stripes ye were healed" - **1 Peter 2:24.**

Christ has paid the ultimate price for my healing and divine health 2000 years ago. I have no reason being sick anymore. Therefore I receive my healing right now, in Jesus name.

---

12. Heavenly Father, let Your healing power go through my veins and entire system right now. Let my body be healed and restored completely, In Jesus name.

---

13. I am healed. Yes. I am healed. I am permanently healed.

In the name of Jesus Christ.

14. (Anoint yourself and pray).

By this anointing, I announce that my healing is sealed, in the heavens, on the earth, and under the earth, in Jesus name

---

15. (Take the communion and pray)

O LORD, my Father.

King of Kings and LORD of lords.

As I take this communion, I am joined to the Body and Blood of Jesus Christ. Whatever cannot afflict Christ has no place in my system.

It is written in Ephesians 2:6 that I am raised up with Christ and seated with Him in the heavenly places, far above all principalities and powers, above sickness and diseases.

LORD Jesus, by eating your flesh and drinking Your Blood, I have eternal life working in me henceforth. (John 6:54).

The life I live now is free from sorrows, sickness and diseases, in Jesus name.

---

16. *O LORD my God, I thank you for my healing.*

Your love and mercy has brought me total healing.

May You be praised forever and ever.

Lord, You have saved me from the lion's mouth. You have delivered me from the wild ox. You have freed me from the devourer's cage.

I shall stand and testify of your goodness before the congregation of your people. (Psalm 22:21-22)

You are the LORD GOD ALMIGHTY. Your praise and glory fills the earth. Your praise fills my life.

In Jesus name.

SECTION 2: PRAYERS OF HEALING FOR LOVED ONES.

(In the blank spaces fill in the name of the person you are praying for)

1. *"Heavenly Father, It is Your will to heal us.*

It is Your will for us to walk in divine health. The price for our healing has been paid on the cross by Your Son, Jesus Christ.

So Father, as I pray for…………………this day, I am confident that Your healing power will be made manifest for his healing and deliverance from the sickness and pain tormenting him, in Jesus name.

2. O LORD, I stand in the gap right now and ask for forgiveness for ....

By the Blood of Jesus I claim forgiveness from any sin and disobedience that has brought or empowered this sickness to operate in the life of ----------------in Jesus name.

3. LORD, You forgive our sins and heal our diseases. Therefore I ask for forgiveness and total healing of this sickness in the life of--------------------in Jesus name.

4. Every spirit that has caused this sickness in ------------------ I command you to get out of his body and be drowned in abyss in Jesus name.

5. Our bodies are the temple of the Holy Spirit. The bodies of .... are the temples of the Holy Spirit.

Therefore, every spirit of defilement in ----, I cast you out right now. This body is not your home. I command you to go into abyss in Jesus name.

6. As I anoint this body, I command a total restoration of health. ----------- be healed in Jesus name.

7. Dear LORD, carry out a Holy Ghost surgery in ....body right now and bring him total healing, in Jesus name

8. Dear Holy Spirit, move into the body of ....and restore every strength and health, In Jesus name.

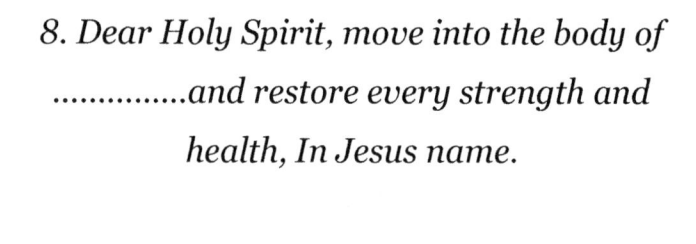

9. I decree that ----------------- will prosper and be in good health, even as the soul prospers in the Lord, in Jesus name.

---

10. Thank You Jesus for healing ....and causing him to walk in divine health. Your work is permanent. Everything you do is perfect.

Thank You Jesus.

Daniel C. Okpara

GOD

BLESS

YOU

Get in Touch

We love testimonies. We love to hear what God is doing around the world as people draw close to Him in prayer. Please share your story with us.

Also, please consider giving this book a review on Amazon and checking out our other titles at: www.amazon.com/author/danielokpara.

I also invite you to checkout our website at www.BetterLifeWorld.org and consider joining our newsletter, which we send out once in a while with great tips, testimonies and revelations from God's Word for a victorious living.

Feel free to drop us your prayer request. We will join faith with you and God's power will be released in your life and the issue in question

Other Books By the Same Author

1. Prayer Retreat: 21 Days Devotional With Over 500 Prayers & Declarations to Destroy Stubborn Demonic Problems.

2. HEALING PRAYERS & CONFESSIONS

3. 200 Violent Prayers for Deliverance, Healing, and Financial Breakthrough.

4. Hearing God's Voice in Painful Moments

5. Healing Prayers: Prophetic Prayers that Brings Healing

6. Healing WORDS: Daily Confessions & Declarations to Activate Your Healing.

7. Prayers That Break Curses and Spells and Release Favors and Breakthroughs.

8. 120 Powerful Night Prayers That Will Change Your Life Forever.

9. How to Pray for Your Children Everyday

10. How to Pray for Your Family

11. Daily Prayer Guide

12. Make Him Respect You: 31 Very Important Relationship Advice for Women to Make their Men Respect them.

13. How to Cast Out Demons from Your Home, Office & Property

14. Praying Through the Book of Psalms

15. The Students' Prayer Book

16. How to Pray and Receive Financial Miracle

17. Powerful Prayers to Destroy Witchcraft Attacks.

18. Deliverance from Marine Spirits

19. Deliverance From Python Spirit

20. Anger Management God's Way

21. How God Speaks to You

22. Deliverance of the Mind

23. 20 Commonly Asked Questions About Demons

24. Praying the Promises of God

25. When God Is Silent! What to Do When Prayer Seems Unanswered or Delayed

26. I SHALL NOT DIE: Prayers to Overcome the Spirit and Fear of Death.

27. Praise Warfare

28. Prayers to Find a Godly Spouse

29. How to Exercise Authority Over Sickness

About the Author

Daniel Chika Okpara is a foremost Christian teacher and author whose books are in high demand in prayer groups, Bible studies, and for personal devotions. He has authored over 50 life-transforming books and manuals on business, prayer, relationship and victorious living, many of which have become international best-sellers on Amazon, Barnes and Noble, Apple Inc., etc.

He is the president and CEO of Better Life World Outreach Center, a non-denominational ministry dedicated to global evangelism, prayer revival and empowering of God's people with the WORD to make their lives better.

He is also the founder of Breakthrough Prayers Foundation (www.breakthroughprayers.org), an online portal leading people all over the world to encounter God and change their lives through prayer. Every day, thousands of people use the Breakthrough Prayers Portal to pray, and hundreds of testimonies from all around the world are received through it.

He is a Computer Engineer by training and holds a Master's Degree in Theology from Cornerstone Christian University. He is married to Doris Okpara, his best friend, and the most significant support in his life. They are blessed with two lovely children.

To connect with him for prayers, counseling, or other issues, visit www.betterlifeworld.org.

NOTES

Printed in Great Britain
by Amazon